AF374638

LIBRARY OF CONGRESS CATALOGING-IN-PUBLICATION DATA
Name: Sellin, Patrick Merle.
Title: My Soul To Keep / Patrick Merle Sellin
Description: Cascadia Bioregion, Sacred Fires Lodge.
First Edition, First Printing, 2023. Self published.
ISBN: 979-8-218-24224-4
Subjects: LCSH: Prose poems, American. |
Mysticism--Poetry. | BISAC: BODY, MIND & SPIRIT /
Inspiration & Personal Growth. | FICTION / Visionary &
Metaphysical. | PHILOSOPHY / Religious.

my soul to keep
BLASPHEMIES & GRATITUDES

PATRICK MERLE SELLIN

HONORING

all thanks to the Giver and Gift
of this Breath, the one I am
flowing in and out with
eternally now,

and to this beloved Earth
with whose trees we breathe
and wisdom we well within–

noble darkness shining,
guide us safely through–

us earthlings
and all beings beyond
these cosmic shores of which
the milky way is just
a salty splash–

for this rarest chance
of remembering what
we really are–

Great Breath of inspiration
from which all form flows,

breathe us now!

now I lay me down to sleep,
I pray the Lord my soul to keep,
guide me safely through the night,
and wake me with the morning light

my soul to keep

guide me safely through

the night

and

wake me with the morning

light

DEDICATION

THE CAIRN (FOR ANDY)

apparently, I erected a cairn at the desert-edge
of my childhood, because I'm standing by it now
again, feeling what that child felt: dehydrated,
lonely; wondering how other children are
faring; if any adults remember
when they lost *their* way.

my favorite color was orange, I thought,
but I always wished it was green.

I had my bags packed once,
sitting outside my family's house,
waiting for the taxicab I called
to show me where home was.
I tied leaves of grass together,
like a crucifix, while I waited:
they wouldn't hold. I think
that's why I finally went inside,
because the crucifix wouldn't hold.

and because it was snack time.
Andy, our shetland sheepdog,
welcomed me back, wished me
better luck next time and
shared my snack.

Andy was always good to me.
it hurt to muzzle him every time
we played basketball. still, he ran
circles around us while we played.
I thought that was courageous.
we had him debarked twice but
his bark always came back;
I knew that was magic.

we ate graham crackers and
gazed out the bay window, thinking
about crying for the boy who wasn't
taking the taxicab. Andy knew I'd find
my way though, so I did too. I stacked
those desert rocks because Andy thought
I should. *feel silenced but live loudly anyway*
is how I would have liked to dedicate the cairn,
but I was just a boy who couldn't
get the crucifix to hold.

most of my other memories are mirages.
I don't know how to talk about them.
I wish I had known the difference
between my family and my soul.
and I really wish we hadn't muzzled
Andy. he knew about the desert and
he never stopped barking about it.
that's why we built the cairn.

PRE FACE

in the beginning,
before we had faces,
we were waves and vibrations.

nowadays,
choices chain us here,
all made-up in our me-masks,

living lives of simple suffocation,
too afraid to breathe without the *me*.

blasphemy!
it's like suffocating
by holding your own breath
—no one can be forgiven for that.

how do we awaken from the apnea?
thankfully— this folk prayer offers a way…

now I lay me down to sleep,
I pray the Lord my soul to keep,
guide me safely through the night,
and wake me with the morning light

…the daily duty of unmasking ourselves.
choice is a freedom we can always make;

midwives of our own beautiful lives. yes—
our souls rest in a beauty that never sleeps.

breather, breathe… …yawn the dawn!
please— stop pretending you're not awake.

now I lay me down to sleep,
I pray the Lord my soul to keep,
guide me safely through the night,
and wake me with the morning light

IT'LL COST YOU

honesty says, I help life
become more of itself
if you let me,

though it'll cost you
every last lie you keep
hidden in your heart

and all the fears you
refuse to talk about
—even to yourself.

if you want to know
eternal life before you die,
it'll cost you everything
that's not truly you.

HOW IT HAPPENS

remember how it happens–

how all that's left is emptiness
folded heavy in your chest as
all your attachments stare
blankly back at you,

how all that's left is looking
for new ways to surrender
as you raise your whitest sail
and set your soul for departure,

how there's no such thing as
answers, only questions
in the form of horizons…

remember how it happens–

how you could *be* anything,
could *believe* anything,
become anything, *anytime;*

how here you always are,
how now it always is, how
love is all that ever is–

and all you were was emptiness.
how sure you were you knew,
before the wind snuck up
behind you.

THE SUN AND YOU

me's the veil that
won't be lifted. it
devils and darkens,
dazzling you with
ideas of identity
you agree to
say yes to.

thankfully, it's the sort
of darkness where
starlight winks
as soon as
you're ready.

it's that easy.
the sun and you
are not so separate.

yes, you chose a path.
it seemed good and right
but now it's a noose.
you can barely breathe

and when you pull away
the grip gets tighter.

that's how you know it's a
trap, if when you pull away,
the grip gets tighter.

yes, it's confusing
and it may feel cruel

that your salve *includes*
the bite it's meant to cure.

STREAM OF SEPARATENESS

I'm afraid of being stuck
and not being true
to my nature,

afraid of damming
or drying up,

of the Tao not being
and my banks eroding.

look at me being
too much of myself
and starting a swamp...

what if I never find the river?

God—
there's nothing so fearful
as not flowing!

A WAY IN

preach your ideas,
sell me all your trinkets;
I'll put them on the shelf
next to everything else
I've ever collected
and called *myself*.

but tell me friend,
what have they to do
with this: the unopened door
of my deepest longing,
much older than *me* or *you*,
the home unseen yet sorely felt
—is this key you peddle a way in?

when my portal appears
amongst the thousands of others
though all may seem more splendid
or necessary than mine, I will
pass over my threshold
alone
and waste my life on
that revelation.

whatever lies on the other side
will be enough, because
nothing of myself
will be left to possess it.

now I lay me down **to sleep**,
I pray the Lord my soul to keep,
guide me safely through the night,
and wake me with the morning light

my new year's resolution
is to fall asleep with
the blinds open.

I want all the fears
that haunt my nights
staring in at me, so they
can see how peacefully
I've learned to rest

and how brave
the love looks
in my eyes when
I stare back at them.

SUNSPOTS

don't you see?

all your shoulds have left you
blinded with deceit,
wondering why
you're still squinting.

you should know better
than to stare into the sun
of your ego's game.

don't you see?

the problems have passed
and it's just beliefs
blazing like sunspots
whose twilight ended
long, long ago.

this dark and aching absence
is the nearest north star
you'll ever know.

when I sit beside this river, I notice
how shallow my being can become,
how hurriedly my mind searches for
the unnatural notion of resolution…

to the left, to the left, to the rising sun
my gaze goes, until some grace
blinds me into contemplation.

a stone
beneath the current
is still, yet its form wavers,
like mine…

ripples
stray to shore—
defiance I never knew
I had; countless moments
to break free from the
flow of myself…

the big montana sky,
too clear-minded to
make observations,
like this rippling
vastness
I now sit as.

many glaciers
have melted
into this river

and so have I.

BENEATH THE BRIDGE

forget the mind that has its doubts
and root down deeper in the now.

beneath the bridge of time
the river joins our many lives.

every death is also birth in breath.
barely here, now barely body,

a new mind bubbles up to be
the love that walks on water.

before the wisdom went away,
elixirs rained and rivered freely.
every human sipped the secret.

now science shows the way
the magic happened:

our voices made mandalas
we could drink. we'd whisper
prayers into purity and drain
away disease. and when
Earth was asked
permission
she'd say,

dig here
and I'll become
a well of revelation.

we've almost forgotten that
two-thirds of our bodies ripple
with prophecies we make ourselves.

someday the stones might say,
remember when the wizards swam
and witches drank their futures
from palms of thankful hands?

remember when the mystics
baptized themselves and
parted seas? remember

when water was sacred and
words were the sacrament?

HOW MANY LIFETIMES

how many lifetimes have droned and
dirged along, breath to death to dust
with too much silence from your soul?

when will the snow owl be spooked
by your life-lamenting howl? how
many half-loves will be wintered
before you risk saying,

I barely understand
and I'm sorry—
but no more.

when will this life be the one
your soul stands enfleshed
on its lonely hill of hell
to scream, *here I am!?*

now I lay me down to sleep,
I pray the Lord my soul to keep,
guide me safely through the night,
and wake me with the morning light

PSALM ONE

hop up to the heart's ledge
and whirl down the river-gorge
of your wild inner landscape.

have a lounge in a grassy shadow
and say aloud what surrender
says you should be.

there
you can meditate
by the red oak tree,
rooted by mossy basalt,
yielding beauty that's in-season
and whose love never withers.

whatever you do, remember:
whatever you love prospers.
not for the fearful—
they are like shadows
papa sun chases away.

therefore, surrender to the law
of your innermost heart, where
the Lord and the Lady run wild
and upon that love-ledge,
promise me— *mediate*,
day and night.

THE WELL OF BEING

you drew me like water
up the well of being
and we drank.

you asked,
which mountain
will we worship from?
I stood still, gazing vastly,
palms wide open:

the time is here
when lovers cease
their worship of nouns.

what gift could be greater
than this thirst
satisfied?

anywhere you lay to breathe
is the source that moves
mountains. I tell you
the truth:

this mountain is you,
this faith is free.

I PASS YOU THIS FEATHER

I pass you this feather, you
who still looks for a sign—
this feather's found us.

something as simple as a
synapse firing's led us here,
a butterfly wing's wind
we feel as a flash of fate
for no foreseeable reason.

I pass you this feather, you
in the darkness of night. *look—*
our heart-lamps, our light!

those shards of distant pain
that surface now, like shingles,
are the fears and shames
our scorpionic souls
refuse to forgive
or let live.

I offer you this mirror
of my presence here, the
black holes of my pupils
reminding you of that
linchpin promise you've
avoided long enough!

this feather of fire waits
for you to feed your name
to all your hungry
shadow shades.

this feather's yours
now. rest awhile
in your nest of
unsavored glories.
dawn your eagle eyes
and soar your heart sky
as soon as you're ready.

A PEARL OF NO PRICE

Jesus spoke of a field where
lovers sell everything they have
for a chance at finding a pearl.

I'm scared, or, *I've made a mistake,*
is what sinners say– those who fret
with fear for all they think they've lost.

notice the flowers of the field: how
they bloom and dance and die, forgiven
by all the birds and bees they leave behind.

Jesus never says how to be as wild
as the flowers, or how to waggle
like a bee imbibing presence.

but maybe someday, laying down
in this field or the next, you'll
have your hand planted
on your chest

and find pulsing there a pearl
too precious to think
of selling.

RESURRECTION

the mission of life
is to truly live
and truly die
many, many times
before you die.

it matters less than you think
who rises up— just love
and die and love
and die and
call it all
my life.

surrender isn't giving up
—it's ceasing to resist
a life that's replacing
what's already lost

and the miracle
is that nothing true
is ever truly lost.

THE BELOVED

your birth was a wedding
arranged by *you*.

you so loved the world
that all the ancestors and
a thousand eager souls
agreed: *this one will
carry our fire forward*.

you knew about your body,
all the shadows in its genes
and all the griefs you'd
wrestle into gifts.

even shame is an ally
announcing where
your gold mine is.

don't you dare believe
you came all this way to
waste your inheritance!

don't you dare believe
the lie of a loyalty to
anything less than
a *fuck yes*!

love is a rose you give yourself
even though you know it's wilting
and life's a way of walking, knowing
wherever you go, the way is blessed.

everywhere you go,
you bring the beloved.

now I lay me down to sleep,
I pray the Lord **my soul to keep**,
guide me safely through the night,
and wake me with the morning light

THE SWITCH

there's a switch inside that's labeled
love. no matter how dark it gets
you can always reach the switch.

when I was a child, my darkest wound
was when my dad turned the light off
while I was still being in the room.

if someone were to see this and
switch that sorrow back to sunlight,
they would have my instant devotion.

CIRCLING

this circling you do
in the drifts of life
is the inner eagle
wading for a gust
that becomes
the new way,

or the wanderer
who makes a
u-turn towards
an expected
boon of fate.

no matter what you do,
when the way appears,
your soul sees
and says,

yes Yes YES
until suddenly
you're soaring!

A SECRET WITHIN

there are valleys we create ourselves,
complete with rivers we cry ourselves and
thoughts for shadows to keep company.

here, the psyche sifts for a sign,
a remnant of life worth refining,
some truth the river lets us
walk off with.

what gets found is a
remembrance, a subtlety,
a wisp of gold inside a stone,
a precious peace within the soul,
within the mind, within
the human body.

when someone asks you
what finally saved you, say,
a friend within a fractal,

a stone
within a river
within a valley I was
when everything I thought I was
seemed lost.

THE FRIEND

life is a breadcrumb trail
of vulnerablities by which
few are led into the wilderness

of becoming whole. feel
the friend inside of you,
the friend of vulnerability,
the friend that knows

it's perfectly safe to die...

...keep feeling the friend,
keep stooping for nourishment
together, keep walking
each other home.

STAKE YOUR CLAIM

there's a way of being that, for you,
won't feel at all like settling.

stake your claim there
and get to building.

HO'OPONOPONO

imagine
you're out surfing
and some thought-wave of
self-judgment swells and
you start anxious-ing,

but
instead of paddling it
you love it into nothing
with a levee of
awareness…

"I'm sorry, please forgive me,
thank you, I love you,"

every time it rushes at you
like that– every single wave
absolutely innocenced
till you're just floating
on a glassy ocean
of aloha.

now I lay me down to sleep,
I pray the Lord my soul to keep,
guide me safely through the night,
and wake me with the morning light

what will happen to the children
when the women run wild and
the men stop rubbing their
manes away? many suffer
their hells already, slack
in the claws of stagnancy.

not I, not we—
our hearts pound primal,
feeling what they feel
every breath of every day,
snarling at anything sleepy.

we jaw up cubs by the scruff
and keep laying them by the river,
waiting only so long for them
to bless themselves

or else we leave.

GRATITUDE THE GRIEF

give gratitude to grief
not because you like it,
but because it birthed
and it needs you now,
like a colicky infant
that's doing its best.

one honest thank you
soothes the grief teeth
and greets the breath back.

this is what it feels like
to be a mortal: you lead
yourself right up to the cliff,

you make your best guess,
then see if the angels like you.
they don't always favor
the fair maiden or the
faithful friend, but the
solace in you says

to fly anyway. lover, listen:
your grief means you loved
or lost before you learned
how. glorious! it's okay to wail.

this gratitude isn't for you—
it's for your freedom.

A DOLPHIN'S VOW

I whistle while I swim, belly up,
a slick gray wave streaking playfully
beneath their domain. I've learned
that life worth living will always be
endangered by predators fallen prey
to weaponizing their own fears.

if I ever become a human,
I will risk being the I am that I am,
whistling amidst a shadowy species of
pirated minds with pronged harpoons.

vulnerability will always be my signature,
the way of wild I am, a malleable form,
always bending and transcending,
always befriending the next
degree of singularity
I am becoming.

BROWN NEEDLES

your fears
are brown needles
tangled up with what's
still green and living.

all you have to do
is reach out, touch them
and watch them lie like
death in the dust.

beyond the field of fear
there's a cliff of blackness,
a necessary uncertainty
that beckons you
closer.

this unknown
is the same chaos
that births the cosmos.

*what we're afraid of has
already happened.*
remember?

only love has the power
to forgive fear and fly
beyond that field.

beloved: whatever's
necessary to feel
love's lifting
—do that!

TRUE TO ITS FLOW

sometimes there's a fork
and the river splits open
to be true to its flow

and sometimes the river
yearns itself together
by that same force.

maybe both forks find a lake
and meet again engorged as
their sun's hot sweat,

remembered once more
in an immense cloud
of unknowing.

all the same, I know

this river leads us home
and all we ever need is
to be true to its flow.

now I lay me down to sleep,
I pray the Lord my soul to keep,
guide me safely through **the night**,
and wake me with the morning light

LOVE MAY SPOOK YOU

the attic of the human mind
will become haunted if
you insist on hanging
out up there.

climb back down the ladder
you escaped by.

love may spook you at first.
so might the sunlight and
the fresh air,

but I promise you,
you're worth it.

PORTALS OF POSSIBILITY

darkness draws over the dome,
a trusty heirloom blanket
tucking Earth in tight,
right up to its alpine chin.

we lay beneath the tapestry
of stars and space and stories, staring
deeper into destinies we keep
only by surrendering.

how did all this come to be—
this moon I rise in your eyes?
this love you bloom in my belly?
this eros raging through our lives?

all this is happening at once:
we blink slowly, breath deepens,
gazes go inward, a winter we trust.
our eyes open, we're summer again!

we roam this land wherever we are,
grinning like best friends do,
scheming up ways to love, gifting
looks of gold back and forth.

do others see how endless this all is,
this realm of surrender and synchronicity?
everywhere we walk is a field that says
how lucky it is to lick our bare feet!

the dream is finally lucid. we rise up
warmly with the blanket, arm and waist,
arm and shoulder, gasping at all
the portals of possibility.

YOU DON'T EXIST

when an eclipse bends time
and you cease to exist,
yet something silver
and sudden still does—

that's the slice of inspiration
you live by. it still hallows you
in fact. life matters because
it splendors your matters.

don't worry when the sky disappears.
it gets even darker than this.

the starlight in you loves it
when you don't exist.

LIMINALITY

when the world becomes
a lifeless night,
a waiting room of
no apparent purpose,
let the silence be
your medicine, your
trusty nightwatch.

such times are no time
for ecstasy or new lines of
conversation, but for solemnity
and gathering wood.

haunt yourself a while.
be horrified by your
own lack of light,
so when the dawn
does indeed rise, you'll
have the humility to
feel its origin
within you.

your dead silence
will raise gifts for others.
the northern lights will prefer
your own backyard.

others may not perceive
the heavenly show,
but they will see
wraiths of color
in your eyes,

will warm their hands
on the fire of your faithful
preparation— *if* you learn
to trust the waiting room.

THERE'S NO RUSH

listen, says the wind. there's no rush.
it's only now that we've arrived.
hush. this grace lingers
longer if you listen…

now I lay me down to sleep,
I pray the Lord my soul to keep,
guide me safely through the night,
and wake me with the morning light

ALREADY LOVE

the only two things
to know about life are:

no matter what you do,
you die someday, and

no matter what you do,
you're already love.

FOUR RELATIONSHIPS

whenever you're alone
with somebody
remember,
there are at *least*
four relationships–

between you and them,
them and themselves,
you and yourself

and between
the universe
learning to
love itself.

HEAVEN'S GATE

when you get to heaven's gate,
you'll hear a voice that says,

yes, you're welcome here,
and, *do you love yourself?*

CHANCES ARE

chances are it doesn't change
unless you choose to love it

and by loving it, the change
begins to choose *through* you.

PILAMAYE

I pledge allegiance to the sun
and all the cells that
sustain me

and to this planet
on which we dance,
one drum, many songs,
indivisible, with
dignity and
gratitude
for all.

now I lay me down to sleep,
I pray the Lord my soul to keep,
guide me safely through the night,
and **wake me with the morning** light

COSMOS IN US

cosmos in us
sleeps, dreaming
some sweet hand strokes
its ageless face awake
each morning.

SUNBEAMS

before the weight of worry
jumps in to bed with me
and all the what-ifs yank
the sheets away, there's
a void of grace where

sunbeams find me.

this is who I am
before I am anything,
unyoked of life and death
and all the thoughts I think,

just a body bathed by dreams,
a perfect roux of breath,
blood and ease.

no matter what the worries say
or how I fight the flames
that guide me through
dreamless planes of sleep,
I know that I remain—

and while fear may darken what
I see, something else blazes
through the blindness to be
the warmth of breath and
grace and sunbeams.

this morning, some new shell
presents itself, naked, etched
by the prophecies made
on its pilgrimage.

I wonder how many nights
this very shell laid lonely
once its mollusk left
home for another

and how many nights
that abandonment
became shelter
for another?

this body here,
this soft fossil,
this rare treasure,
this wrinkled prayer,
this perfect account of
imperfection, this wayfarer
and dredger of the depths or
wherever love let it wander–

how many prayers will waste
and weep around the spiral
before I find home again,
like this shell, naked
and content with
not knowing?

it seems that time itself
must fall asleep and
become a windy river,
that summer leaves
must flail and scream
all their secrets to
the lovers about the
love they've been given,

about how rare
and perfect
this all is

and how little time remains
to fashion something new
and ancient and inward
and simply inhabitable

—like this shell
that found me
starting all over
again this morning.

GOLDEN TEACHER

pass up the gold ring
that isn't yours and
gather cedar instead.

sweetness on the path
is far more regal than
bling on the finger.

imagine the wealth of
never having more
than you need...

this freedom isn't free:
don't forget to offer a
breath for the trees.

FLOWER OF THE FLESH

the flower of the flesh
is love's lens manifest.
if we bow to the body
and offer her breath,

she blooms for us,
she wafts wisdoms,
she heals, she's whole,
she already knows!

the one who seeks a savior
is already holding her.

you can stay
curled up there
in the cave of your
first impression, or
venture further
into coves of
curiosity

I know—
you have a plan
and it's a good one
and all you need
is a little more
time…

but
the time
for glory is *now*,
your throne is near
and you could be sunlight
leaping thru the forest
to find your seat!

is all this beauty
destiny or delirium?

the answer's there in
the eagles giggling,
the bears gorging
boysenberries
into sunsets
for you.

sure—
you could be
a kitten, cute and
clumsy in the comfort
of the day, languid
in the purring
white light

or,
you could be
a portal where lions
come to consummate
and roar rainbows
through the night.

please,
please burst
into ecstasy for us!

we know that's what
you're doing here—
playing coy until
you become a
supernova.

now I lay me down to sleep,
I pray the Lord my soul to keep,
guide me safely through the night,
and wake me with the morning **light**

HOLY GROUND

holy ground is wherever
you take your shoes off
and feel the humus
pressing cosmic
codes of hope
in your toeprints,

where the humblest heights
of your gorgeous form
kiss the bits of
this eden-Earth,

though all most ever see
are footprints where
others tend not to walk.

PRAYER FLAGS

souls, flagged with flesh, stitched
in time, a brief flapping, just
for the thrill of it

HUMANESSENCE

sun mind, moon mind—
essence inflecting presence
reflecting essence— what
joyful humanessence!

no blackness in the body
breath cannot becandle,
no caverns of the self
love does not enhallow.

breather, *breathe*—
between vibrations,
atomic liberations,
seismic transformations,

attuning up the spine,
purifying mind,
embodied
breath divine!

BURDEN IS BEAUTY

come to me, all who ache
and groan for grace and
I will kiss your face.

be sane and soulful, like
a seed; do not dement the
darkness, nor the breath
from the underground,

for your burden is beauty
and laden with light.

BEHOLD AND HELD

to behold in love
is to be held in love;

to receive this gift
is to be what's gifted;

we do not fall in love
—we are lifted!

JUST THIS ONCE

this is not a dream
you'll dream again

and someday death
will whisk you away
to wherever it is
you came from.

all the stars conspired
to make a home *in* you
and somehow formed
a fire that yearns

just like you,
just this once.

now I lay me down to sleep,
I pray the Lord my soul to keep,
guide me safely through the night,
and wake me with the morning light